SCARY MAZES

William Potter
Leo Trinidad

WINDMILL
BOOKS

Published in 2019 by Windmill Books,
an Imprint of Rosen Publishing
29 East 21st Street, New York, NY 10010

Written by: William Potter
Illustrated by: Leo Trinidad
Designed by: Stefan Holliland with Emma Randall
Edited by: Joe Harris with Julia Adams

Cataloging-in-Publication Data

Names: Potter, William. | Trinidad, Leo, illustrator.
Title: Scary mazes / William Potter; illustrated by Leo Trinidad.
Description: New York : Windmill Books, 2019. | Series: Ultimate finger trace mazes | Includes glossary and index.
Identifiers: ISBN 9781538390061 (pbk.) | ISBN 9781508197263 (library bound) | ISBN 9781538390078 (6 pack)
Subjects: LCSH: Maze puzzles--Juvenile literature.
Classification: LCC GV1507.M3 T756 2019 | DDC 793.73'8--dc23

Manufactured in the United States of America

CPSIA Compliance Information: Batch BW19WM: For Further Information contact Rosen Publishing, New York, New York at 1-800-237-9932

CONTENTS

HOW TO USE THIS BOOK

This book is full of high-risk mazes, where you have to help the heroes find a safe path to complete their daring missions. Look out! Every page is packed with perils.

1. READ THE INSTRUCTIONS CAREFULLY BEFORE USING YOUR FINGER TO GUIDE THE HEROES FROM THE START TO THE FINISH.

2. AVOID ALL THE DANGERS. MAKE SURE THE HEROES AREN'T TRAPPED, ZAPPED, OR SNAPPED UP FOR LUNCH!

SAVE ME!

START HERE!

ESCAPE

3. OFTEN, SOMEONE NEEDS RESCUING. LEAD THE HEROES THERE FIRST, BEFORE HELPING THEM TO ESCAPE!

4. YOU CAN FIND THE SOLUTIONS TO ALL THE MAZES FROM PAGES 26 TO 29.

SWIM TO SHORE

The swim to the beach is full of peril. Find a safe route without touching rocks, spiky urchins, or grabby crabs.

START HERE!

EXIT

DIVE of DooM

Swim through the octopus arms to free the desperate diver caught on the seabed, then guide him toward the surface.

ESCAPE!

START HERE!

HELP!

DON'T WAKE THE LIONS!

Our heroes are trapped in the zoo's lion enclosure. Help them tiptoe to the key, and get out without tripping over sleeping lions or their food.

START

KEY

HIGH RISK

Use the ladders and ropes to climb this Himalayan peak while avoiding the angry animals and yeti.

FEELING THE HEAT

The volcano's ready to erupt. Race to pick up your monitoring equipment, and book it to the rescue chopper before things get too hot!

DINO DASH

The time explorers are in the age of dinosaurs. Help them dash to their time machine without becoming lunch.

START HERE!

EXIT

WILD WOLVES

This winter walker needs to get out of the forest fast because the wolf pack is on his trail. Show him the path to the snowmobile.

START HERE!

EXIT

RAMPART RESCUE

The brave knight needs to rescue her princely brother from the tower, and escape without fighting the troll guards. How will she do it?

MOON MAZE

The two astronauts are low on air. They must hurry to their moon buggy, dodging rocks, scalding-hot bubbles, and hungry alien creatures.

MOON BUGGY

START HERE!

CHILLER THRILLER

The Ice Age cave people need to find a safe path over the snow to their frozen cave–without waking the mammoths!

HOME

START HERE!

18

DANGER DAM

The dam is about to burst! Help the two visitors over the top, avoiding cracks. Quick!

EXIT

START HERE!

CHAIN CHALLENGE

A friendly dragon has been captured by grumpy goblins. Carry the key up the chain to the lock to free him.

UNLOCK CHAIN

START HERE!

20

LOST LUGGAGE

A poor pup is lost in the airport baggage claim. Find a way over the conveyor to him, without bumping into any suitcases.

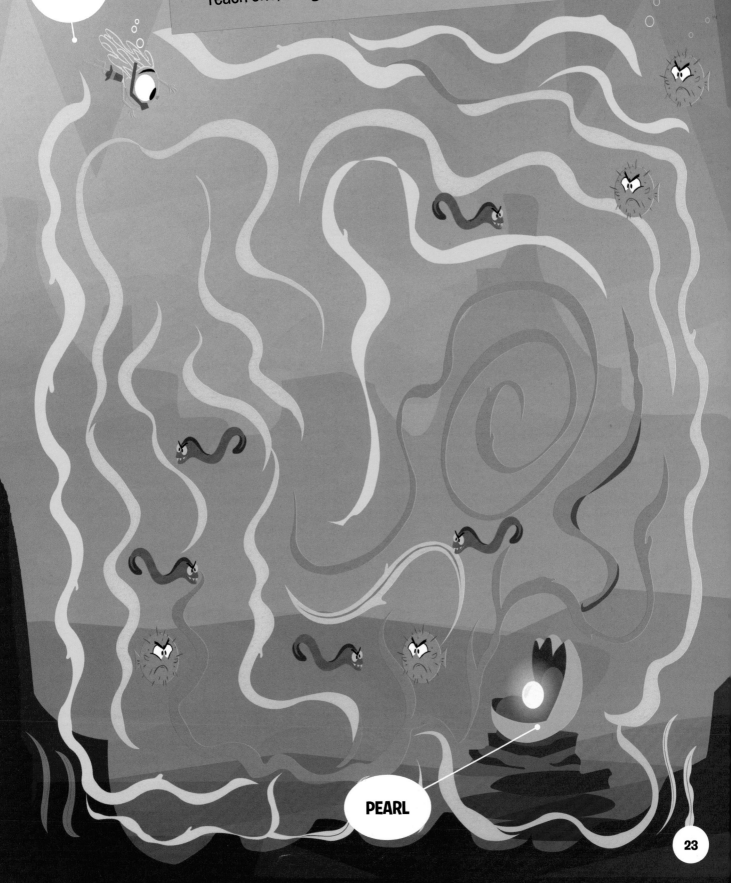

EGG ESCAPE

No eggs for breakfast! Get away from the giant bird nest. Quick, the mother bird looks angry!

START HERE!

ESCAPE

24

SCARY MAZES
SOLUTIONS

PAGE 5

PAGE 6

PAGE 7

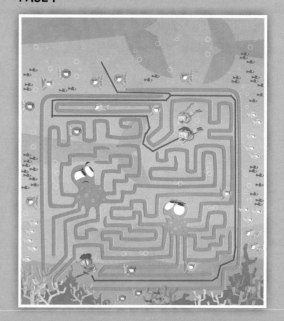

PAGE 8

PAGE 9

PAGE 10

PAGE 11

PAGE 12

PAGE 13

PAGE 14

PAGE 15

PAGE 16

PAGE 17

PAGE 18

PAGE 19

PAGE 20

PAGE 21

PAGE 22

PAGE 23

PAGE 24

PAGE 25

GLOSSARY

ape A type of primate that doesn't have a tail, such as gorillas and chimpanzees.

conveyor A belt that moves, transporting luggage for passengers to retrieve.

enclosure An area that is fenced.

equipment Tools for a particular job.

gator Short for "alligator."

Ice Age A period of time when much of Earth was covered in glaciers.

kelp A type of seaweed.

larva (plural–larvae) The young, immature form of insects.

mammoth An extinct prehistoric animal that looked like a huge, hairy elephant with long tusks.

menace A threat or danger.

peril Serious danger.

rampart A castle's defensive wall.

seabed The ground under an ocean or sea.

snowmobile A vehicle that is designed to travel fast over snow.

urchin A spiky sea creature.

FURTHER INFORMATION

Books:

Kamigaki, Hiro. *Pierre the Maze Detective: The Search for the Stolen Maze Stone.* London, UK: Laurence King Publishing, 2017.

Robson, Kirsteen. *Pirate Maze Book.* London, UK: Usborne Publishing, 2016.

Smith, Sam. *Map Maze Book.* London, UK: Usborne Publishing, 2015.

Wilson, Becky. *Totally Amazing Mazes: 100 Twisty Turny Adventures.* Bath, UK: Parragon, 2015.

Websites:

For web resources related to
the subject of this book, go to:
www.windmillbooks.com/weblinks
and select this book's title.

INDEX

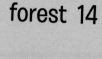